Arthur

EARLY ENGLISH TEXT SOCIETY

Original Series, No. 2

1864 (second edition 1869;

reprinted 1965)

PRICE 7*s*. 6*d*.

Arthur

A SHORT SKETCH OF HIS LIFE AND HISTORY IN ENGLISH VERSE

EDITED FROM

THE MARQUIS OF BATH'S MS.

LIBER RUBEUS BATHONIÆ, 1428 A.D.

BY

FREDERICK J. FURNIVALL

Published for

THE EARLY ENGLISH TEXT SOCIETY

by the

OXFORD UNIVERSITY PRESS

LONDON NEW YORK TORONTO

OXFORD
UNIVERSITY PRESS

Great Clarendon Street, Oxford OX2 6DP
United Kingdom

Oxford University Press is a department of the University of Oxford.
It furthers the University's objective of excellence in research, scholarship,
and education by publishing worldwide. Oxford is a registered trade mark of
Oxford University Press in the UK and in certain other countries

First Edition published in 1864
Second Edition 1869
Reprinted 1965, 1998

Published in the United States of America by Oxford University Press
198 Madison Avenue, New York, NY 10016, United States of America

British Library Cataloguing in Publication Data
Data available

Library of Congress Cataloging in Publication Data
Data available

Original Series, 2

ISBN 978-0-85-991800-8

PREFACE.

As one of the chief objects of the Early English Text Society is to print every Early English Text relating to Arthur, the Committee have decided that this short sketch of the British hero's life shall form one of the first issue of the Society's publications. The six hundred and forty-two English lines here printed occur in an incomplete Latin Chronicle of the Kings of Britain, an abbreviation of the *Brut*, bound up with many other valuable pieces in the *Liber Rubeus Bathoniæ*, 1428 A.D.,[1] belonging to the Marquis of Bath. The old chronicler has dealt with Uther Pendragon, and is narrating Arthur's deeds,—telling of the siege of Bath, of Brou*n*steell (Excalibur) '*caliburni, gladii Arthuri*,' of the conquest of Scotland, Ireland, Gothland, and the founding of the *Rotunda Tabula*, made round that none should be above, none below, but all sit equal—when, as if feeling that Latin prose was no fit vehicle for telling of Arthur, king of men, he breaks out into English verse,

> "Herkeneþ, þat loueþ hon*our*,
> Of kyng Arthour & hys lab*our*."

The story he tells is an abstract, with omissions, of the earlier version of Geoffry of Monmouth, before the love of Guinevere for Lancelot was introduced by the French-writing

[1] This is the date on the back of the case of the MS.

English romancers of the Lionheart's time (so far as I know), into the Arthur Tales. The fact of Mordred's being Arthur's son, begotten by him on his sister, King Lot's wife, is also omitted; so that the story is just that of a British king founding the Round Table, conquering Scotland, Ireland, Gothland, and divers parts of France, killing a giant from Spain, beating Lucius the Emperor of Rome, and returning home to lose his own life, after the battle in which the traitor whom he had trusted, and who has seized his queen and his land, was slain.

> "He that will more look,
> Read on the French book"

says our verse-writer: and to that the modern reader must still be referred, or to the translations of parts of it, which we hope to print or reprint, and that most pleasantly jumbled abstract of its parts by Sir Thomas Maleor, Knight, which has long been the delight of many a reader,—though despised by the stern old Ascham, whose Scholemaster was to turn it out of the land.—There the glory of the Holy Grail will be revealed to him; there the Knight of God made known; there the only true lovers in the world will tell their loves and kiss their kisses before him; and the Fates which of old enforced the penalty of sin will show that their arm is not shortened, and that though the brave and guilty king fights well and gathers all the glory of the world around him, yet still the sword is over his head, and, for the evil that he has done, his life and vain imaginings must pass away in dust and confusion.

Of the language of the Poem there is little to say: its dialect is mostly Southern, as shown by the verbal plural *th*, the *vyve* for five, *zyx* for six, *ych* for I, *har* (their), *ham* (them), for *her, hem; hulle, dude, ȝut*, for hill, did, yet, the infinitive in *y* (*rekeny*), etc.; but Northern forms appear, as *fra*, from (l. 628), *at*, that (l. 640). Of its poetical merits, every reader will judge for himself; but that it has power in some parts I hope few will deny. Arthur's answer to Lucius, and two lines in the duel with Frollo,

> "There was no word y-spoke,
> But eche had other by the throte,"

are to be noted. Parts of the MS. have very much faded since it was written some ten or twenty years before 1450, so that a few of the words are queried in the print. The MS. contains a few metrical points and stops, which I have here printed between parentheses ( ). The expansions of the contractions are printed in italics, but the ordinary doubt whether the final lined *n* or *u*—for they are often undistinguishable—is to be printed n*e*, n*ne*, *u*n, or u*n*, exists here too. I have generally printed it n̄.

I am indebted to Mr Sims, of the Manuscript Department of the British Museum, for pointing out the Poem to me, and to the Marquis of Bath for his kind permission to copy it for printing.

Old Square, Lincoln's Inn,
London, W.C., August 30, 1864.
(*Revised, March* 2, 1869.)

ARTHUR,

FROM THE MARQUIS OF BATH'S MS.

1428 A.D.

[The Latin side-notes in italics and Clarendon, and the stops of the text in parentheses ( ), are those of the MS.]

HErkenoþ, þat loueþ hono*ur*,
Of kyng Arthour & hys labo*ur*;
And furst how he was bygete,
As þ*at* we in bok*is* do rede.
Vther pendragoñ was hys fader,
And ygerne was hys Moder.
Pendragoñ ys in walysch̄
'Dragones heed' on Englysch̄
He maked ypeynted dragoñs two;
Oon schold[1] byfore him goo
Whan he went to batayle,
Whan he wold hys foes sayle;
That other abood at wynchester,
Euer-more stylle there.
Bretones ȝaf hym þ*at* Name,
Vther Pendragoñ þe same,
For þat skyle fer & nere
Euer-more hyt to bere.
¶
The Erles wyff of Cornewayle
He loued to Muche sanȝ fayle;

[leaf 42, back]

How Arthur was begotten by Pendragon on Ygerne.

Pendragon (*t.i.* Dragon's Head) made two painted dragons, and thence had his name.

How Uther loved the Earl of Cornwall's wife,

[1] 'scold' over an erasure in the text; 'schold' in the left margin.

Merlyn wyþ hys sotelnesse
Turned vtheris lyknesse,
And maked hym lyche þe Erl anone,
And wyþ hys wyff (:) his wyƚƚ to done
In þe co*u*ntre of Corneweƚƚ :
In þe Castel of Tyntageƚƚ,
Thus vther, yf y schaƚƚ nat lye,
Bygat Arthour in avowtrye. — *and begat Arthur in adultery.*
Whan vther Pendragon̄ was deed,
Arthour anon was y-crowned ; — *Arthur is crowned,*
He was courteys, large, & Gent
To alle puple verrament ;
Beaute, Myȝt, amyable chere
To alle Men ferre and neere ;
Hys port (;) hys ȝyftes gentyƚƚ
Maked hym y-loved wyƚƚ ; — *is loved of all,*
Ech mon was glad of hys p*re*sence,
And drade to do hym dysplesan̄ce ;
A stronger Man of hys honde — *is strong*
was neuer fou*n*de on any londe,
As courteys as any Mayde :— — *and courteous.*
þus wryteþ of hym þ*at* hym a-sayde.
At Cayrlyon̄ w*y*t*h*oute fable, — [leaf 42 bk, col. 2.]
He let make þe Rou*n*de table : — *He makes the Round Table,*
And why þ*at* he maked hyt þus,
þis was þe resou*n* y-wyss,—
þat no man schulde sytt aboue other, — *that all at it might be equal.*
Ne haue indignacio*u*n of hys broþ*er* ;
And alle hadde (.)oo(.) seruyse,
For no pryde scholde aryse
For any degree of syttynge,
Oþer for any seruynge :
þus he kept þe table Rou*n*de
Whyle he leuyd on þe gro*u*nde.
After he hadde conquered Skotlond — *After his first conquests*
Yrland & Gotland,

þan leuyd he at þe best
he lives twelve years in peace,
Twelf ȝeeris on alle reste
Wyþoute werre (:) tyll at þe laste
He þouȝt to make (.)a(.) nywe conquestc.
Into Fraunce wyþ gode counceyle
and then invades France.
he wolde weende (:) & hyt assayle,
þat Rome þo kept vnder Myght,
Vnder Frollo (:) a worthy knyght
þat fraunce hadde þo to kepe,
To rywle, defende, & to lede.
Arthour and Frollo fowȝt in feld;
He beats Frollo back to Paris,
þere deyde many vnder scheld.
Frollo in-to Paryss fly,
Wyth strenkthe kept hyt wysely:
Arthour byseged þat Syte & town
and there besieges him, till.
Tyll þeire vytayl was y-doon.
Frollo þat worthy knyght
Frollo challenges him to single combat.
Proferyd wyth Arthour for to fyght
Vnder þis wyse & condicioun,—
"Ho hadde þe Maystrie (:) haue þe crown;
And no mo men but þey two."
þe day was sett (:) to-geder' þey go:
They fight:
Fayr hyt was to byholde
In suche two knyȝghteȝ bolde:
þer was no word y-spoke,
But eche hadde other by þe þrote;
þey smote wyth trounchoun & wyth swerd;'.
þat hyt seye, were a-ferd;
[leaf 48.]
Frollo fowȝt wyþ hys ax (:) as men dude se;
(Frollo with his axe)
He hytt Arthour (:) so sore (:) þat he felle on kne.
He ros vp raply (:) and smot hym full sore;
He dude hym to grent a (.) soueȝ[1] þerfore.
[1 ? soneȝ]
Thus they hyw on helmes hye,
And schatered on wyþ scheldes.
þe puple by-gan to crye
þat stood on þe feldes;

Ther ne wyst no man, as y can lere,
Who of ham two was þe bettere þere.

till Arthur in wrath takes Brownsteel,

Arthour was chafed & wexed wroth̄,
He hente broun*n*steeƚƚ / and to Frollo goth̄ ;

*Caliburn*us *Arthuri Gladius* [with a sketch thereof in the MS.] and strikes Frollo dead.

Broun*n*steƚƚ was heuy & also kene ;
Fra*m* þe schulder (:) to þe syde went bytwene
Off frollo / and þan he fell to þe grou*n*de
Ry3t as he moste / deed (.) in lyte stou*n*de.
Frensch̄ men made doeƚƚ & wept fuƚƚ faste ;
Þeir Crowne of frau*n*ce þere þey loste.

Arthur takes Paris.

Than wente Arthour in-to paryse
And toke þe casteƚƚ & þe town at hys avyse.

Glory to God.

Worschuped be god of hys grete grace
Þ*at* þus 3eueþ fortune (:) and worschup to þe Reme ;
Thanke 3e hym aƚƚ þ*at* beþ on þis place,

Say ye a Pater Noster therefore.

And seyeþ a Pater noster w*yth*out any Beeme.
¶ // *Pater noster.* //
Artho*ur* fram Paryse went w*yth* hys Rowte,

Arthur conquers the countries around,

And co*n*quered þe Cõtre on euery syde aboute ;
Angeoy,[1] Peytow, Berry, & Gaskoyne,
Nauerne, Burgoñ / Loreyn & Toreyne ;
He dau*n*ted þe proude / & hawted þe poure ;
He dwelt long in Paryss after in honoure ;
He was drad and loued in cõtreis abowte ;
Heyest & lowest hym Loved & alowte ;
And vp-on an Esto*ur* tyme sone afterward

distributes them among his knights,

He fested hys knyght*is* & 3af ham gret reward ;
To hys Styward he 3af Angers & Añgeye ;
To Bedewer hys botyler he 3af Norma*n*dye ;
He 3af to Holdyne flau*n*drys parde ;
To Borel hys Cosyn, Boloyne þe Cyte ;
And eche man, after þe astat þat he was,
He rewarded hem alle, boþe More & lasse,
And 3af hem reward, boþe lond and Fee,

and returns to Britain.

And turned to Breteyn, to Carlyoñ ayhe.

[1] ? MS. perhaps *Angecye*. See *Angeoy*, l. 312.

[lf. 43 bk, col. 1.]

Arthur gives an Easter Feast

Arth*our* wolde of hono*ur*
Hold a fest at Eestour
Of regalye & worthynesse,
And feede alle hys frendess;
And sende Messanger
To kynges ferre & neer
þat were to hym Omager,
to come to þis Dyner.
And alle at oo certeyn day
They come þyder in gode aray,
And kept þeire Cesoñ
At þe Castełł Carlyoñ.
Thys fest was Muche Moore
þan euere Arth*our* made a-fore;
For þere was Vrweyn þe kynge
Of scottes at þat dynynge,
Stater þe kyng of south wales,
Cadwełł þe kyng of north waleȝ,
Gwylmar þe kyng of yrland,
Dolmad þe kyng of guthland,
Malgan of yselond also,
Archyl of De*n*march þ*er*to,
Aloth̄ þe kyng of Norwey,
Souenas þe kyng of Orkenye,
Of Breteyn þe kyng Hoel,
Cador Erl of Cornewełł,
Morice þe Erl of Gloucestr*e*,
Marran Erl of Wy*n*chestre,
Gwergo*u*nd Erl of herford,
Booȝ Erl of Oxenford,
Of bathe vngent þe Erl also,
Cursal of Chestr*e* þer-to,
Euerad Erl of Salesbury,[1]
Kynmar Erl of Canterbury,
Ionas þe Erl of Dorcestre,

at Carlyon, greater than ere before.

Ten kings were there,

and thirteen earls

(including him of Bath),

[1] The *s* is rubbed: the word may be "onlesbury."

Valence þe Erl of Sylchestr*e*,
Iugeyn of Leyccer [?] þ*er*to,
Argal of warwyk also,—
Kynges & Erles Echon
with many other gentles great,
þes wer*e*; & many anoþ*er* goom
Gret of astaat, & þe beste,
þes were at þe Feste.
[lf. 43 bk, col. 2.]
Other also gentyls grete
Were þere at þat Meete,
Sauer appon Donand,
Regeym & Alard,
Reyneȝ fitȝ Colys,
Tade*us* fitȝ Reis,
Delyn fitȝ Dauid,
Kymbelyn le fitȝ Gryffitħ,
Gryffitȝ þe sone of Nagand,
þes were þer*e* also theoband:
Alle þes were þer*e* w*yth*oute fable,
besides the Round Tablers,
W*yth*oute ham of þe rou*n*de table.
Archbishops,
Thre archebusschopes þ*er* were also,
Bishops,
And other busschopes many mo—
Aƚƚ þis mayne were nat al-oone;
W*yth* ham com many a Goome.
þis feste dured dayes þre
In reueƚƚ & sole*m*pnite.
and many from beyond the sea.
Of byȝonde þe See also
Many lordeȝ were þere þo.
Now resteþ alle wyþ Me,
And say a Pater & Aue.

¶ **Pater noster.**

The þrydde day folowyng
The*n* coom nywe tydynge,
þe whyle þey sete at þe Mete
To the feasters came messengers from the Roman Emperor,
Messagers were In ylete;
Weƚƚ arayd forsoþe þey come,
Y-send fram cite of Rome

Wyþ l*ett*res of þe Emp*er*oures
Whas name was Lucies.

*Luci*us.

þes l*ett*res were opened & vnfold,
And þe tydyng' to alle men told,
Whas sentence, yf y ne lye,
Was after þ*at* y can aspye:

L*ite*ra Lucii i*mperato*r*is*.

¶ Luci*us* þe grete Emp*er*our
To hys Enemy Arthour :—
We woñdereþ of þi wodeness
And also of þy Madnesse!
How darst þow any wyse
A3enst the Emp*erour* þ*us* aryse,
And ryde on Remes on eche wey,
And make kyngė3 to þe obey?
þu art wood on þe Nolle!
þu hast Scley owre cosyn frolle;

saying, that to have invaded France, etc., and made kings, Arthur must be mad in his noll;

þu schalt be taw3t at a schort day
for to make sucħ aray.

[leaf 44, col. 1.]

Oure cosyn Iuli*us* cesar
So*m*me tyme conquered þar;
To Rome þu owest hys trybut;
We chargeþ þe to paye vs hyt.

that he must pay his tribute,

Thy pryde we wolł alaye
þat makest so gret aray:
We co*m*mandeþ þe on haste
To paye owre trybut faste;
þu hast scley frolle in frau*n*ce
þat hadde vnder vs þere goue*r*nau*n*ce,
And wyþholdest oure tribute þ*er*to:
þu schalt be taw3t þu hast mysdo:
We co*m*mandeþ þe in haste soone
þ*at* þu come to vs at Rome
To vnd*er*fang oure ordynau*n*ce
For þy dysobediau*n*ce;
As þu wold nat le3e þy lyf,
Fulfylle þys w*y*t*h*oute stryff."

and come to Rome to be punished for his disobedience.

(¶ . . . . . ¶ . . . . . ¶ . . . . . ¶)

¶ Whan þis l*ett*re was open & rad,
The Britons purpose to kill the messengers,
Þe bretoñs & aƚƚ men wer*e* mad,
And wolde þe messager scle :—
but Arthur forbids it,
"Nay," seyd Arthour, "per de,
That were aȝenst aƚƚ kynde,
A messager to bete or bynde ;
Y charge alle men here
For to make ham good chere."
And after Mete sanȝ fayl
Wyþ hys lordes he hadde cou*n*sayl ;
And alle asented þer-to,
and resolves to invade Rome.
Artho*ur* to Rome scholde go ;
And þey ne wolde in hys t*ra*uayle
Wyþ strenkþ & good neu*er* fayle.
Than Artho*ur* wroot to Rome a l*ett*re,
Was sentence was so*m*m-what byttere,
And seyde i*n* þis manere
As ȝe may hure here :—

Litera Regis Arthuri.
Arthur's answer to the Emperor Lucius,

"KNoweþ weƚƚ ȝe of Romayne,
Y am kyng Artho*ur* of Bretayne.
Frañce, y haue conquered hyt,
[leaf 44, col. 2.]
Y schaƚƚ defende & kepe hyt ȝut,
Y come to Rome, as y am tryw,
claiming tribute from him.
To take my trybut (.) to me dywe,
But noon þere for to paye,
By my werk ȝe schaƚƚ asay ;
For þe Emp*er*our Constantyne
Þat was þe Soone of Elyne,
Þat was a Bretoñ of þis lond,
Co*n*quered Rome w*y*t*h* hys hond,
And so ȝe oweþ me tribut :
Y charge ȝow þ*at* ȝe pay me hyt.
¶
Also Maximian kyng of Bretai*n*gne
Co[*n*]quered al frañce & Almayne,
Lombardye, Rome, & ytalye—

By ȝoure bok*is* ȝe may a-spye.
Y am þeir Eyr & þeyre lynage,
Y aske ȝow my trywage."

Þis le*tt*re was celyd fast,
Y-take the Messagereȝ on hast;
Arthour ȝaf ham ȝyfteȝ grete,
And chered ham wyþ drynk and Mete.

Lucius's messengers return to him,

Þey hasted ham to come hoom;
Byfor þe Emp*erour* þey beþ coom;
Saluted hym as resoñ ys,
And toke hym þes letterys.
Þey seyde to þe Emp*er*our
"We have be wyþ kyng Artho*ur*;
But such anoþ*er* as he ys oon,
Say neuer no Man.
He ys s*er*ued on hys howshold
Wyþ kynges, Erles, worthy & bold;
Hys worthynesse, sur Emp*er*our,
Asseþ Much all ȝowre;
He seyde he wolde hyder come

and give him Arthur's message.

And take trywage of all Rome,
We dowteþ last he wol do soo,
For he ys Myghty ynow þer-too."
Now, erst þan we goo ferþer,
Every man þat ys here
Sey a Pater noster
And ave wyþ gode chere. Ame*n*.

¶ Pater noster

Ave Maria.

[leaf 44, back.]

Arthur prepares for his expedition to Rome.

Now stureth hym self Artho*ur*
Þenkyng on hys labo*ur*,
And gaderyþ to hym strenghth aboute,
Hys kynges & Erles on a rowte—
A fayr syȝt to Mannes ye
To see such a cheualrye,—

Has five kings,

The kyng of Gotland,
Also þe kyng of Irland,
The kyng of ysland / & of Orkenye,
þis was worthy Maynye;
The kyng' of Denmark also was þere,
þis was a worthy chere:
Eche of þese vyve at her venyw
Brouȝt zyx þousand at har retenyw;

with 30,000 men,

xxx^{ti}. þowsand, yc*h* vnderstand,
þes vyf kyng*is* hadde on honde.

80,000 Normans and

Than hadde he out of Normandye,
Of Angeoy & of Almanye,
Boloyne (.) Peytow & flau*n*dres
Fowre skore þowsand harneys—

12,000 from Chartres,

Geryn of Charteȝ .xij. þowsand
þat went wyþ Arto*ur* euer at honde;

10,000 Bretons,

Hoel of bretayn, þowsandeȝ ten
Of hardy & weƚƚ fyghtyng Men;
Out of Bretaygne hys owne land

and 40,000 British:

He passed fourty þowsand
Of Archerys & off Arblastere
þ*at* Cowþ weƚƚ þe craft of werre.
¶ In Foot other Many a Man Moo
Able to feyghte (:) as weƚƚ as þo:

in all 200,000.

Two hunderd þousand
Went wyþ hym out of lond,
And Many moo sykerly
That y can nat nombrye.
Artho*ur* toke þan þe lond

Britain is left in Mordred's charge.

To Moddredes owne hond;
He kept al oþer þyng
Saue þe Corowne weryng;
But he was [fals] of hys kepynge,
As ȝe schaƚƚ hure here folewynge.

Arthur ships at Southampton,

Now thañ ys Arto*ur* y-Come,
And hys Ost, to Sowthamptone:

Ther was Many a Man of Myghte ¶ Ascend*ebat* naue*m* sua*m* Hamptonie.
Strong & bold also to fyghte.
Eche man hath take his schuppynge, [leaf 44 bk, col. 2.]
And ys at hys loghynge.
Vp goþ þe sayl (:) þey sayleþ faste:
Arthour owt of syȝt ys paste.
þe ferst lond þat he gan Meete,
Forsoþ hyt was Bareflete; *and lands at Barfleet.*
Ther he gan vp furst aryve.
Now weƚƚ Mote Arthou*r* spede & thryve!
And þat hys saule spede þe better, *God speed him!*
Lat eche man sey a pater noster.

¶ Pater noster.

Now god spede Artour weƚƚ!
Hym ys comyng a nyw bateƚƚ. *A new foe appears, a Spanish Giant,*
Ther coom a gyant out of spayne,
And rauasched had fayr Elayne;
He had brouȝt heor' vp on an hulle—
Mornyng hyt ys to hure or telle—
Cosyn heo was to kyng Hoell,
A damesel fayr and genteƚƚ;
And ȝut ferþ*er*more to,
He rauasched heore Moder also. *who has slain fair Elayne.*
He dude þe damesel for to dye,
For he myght not lygge heor' bye.
Whan þis was told to Artour,
He maked Much dolour,
And send Bedewer for to spye *Arthur sends Bedwere first as a spy,*
How he myght come hym bye;
And he was nat Sclowh,
But to þe hulle hym drowh
þat Closed was wyþ wat*er* stronge,
þe hulle a-Mydde gret & longe;
He went ouer to þe hulle syde,
And þere a fonde a wom*m*an byde,
þat sorwedd & wept Mornynge

For Eleynes deþ & dep*ar*tynge,
And bad Bedewer to fle also
Last he were ded more to;
"For yf þe Gyant fynde þe,
W*yth*oute dowte he wyƚƚ þe scle."
Bedwer wyþ aƚƚ hastynge
Tolde Arthou*r* aƚƚ þis þynge.
Amorwe whan þat hyt was day
Arthour toke þyder hys way, — and then (with Bedwere and Key) starts on his adventure.
Bedewer wyþ hym wente, & keye,— [leaf 45]
Men þat cowþe weƚƚ þe weye,—
And broute Arthou*r* Meyntenan̄t
Euen [1] byfore þe gyant. — [1 *by* in a later hand, above.]
Arthour fowȝt wyþ þat wyght;
He had almost ylost hys Myght:
Wyþ Muche peyne, þruȝ goddeȝ g*ra*ce
He sclowh þe Geant in þat place, — He kills the Giant,
And þan he made Bedewere
To smyte of hys heed þere.
To þe Ost he dude hyt brynge,
And þ*er*on was gret won̄drynge,
Hyt was so oryble & so greet, — whose horrible head is shown to the host,
More þan̄ any Horse heed.
Than hadde hoel Ioye ynowh
For þat Arthour so hym sclowh;
And for a p*er*petuel Memorie
He Made a chapeƚƚ of seynt Marye — and St. Mary's Chapel is built in honour of the victory.
In þe hulle vpon þe pleyne,
Wyþ-Inne þat (:) þe t*um*be of Eleyne; — to*m*be.
And þat name wyþoute nay
Hyt bereþ ȝut in-to þis day.
Now ys an ende of þis þynge,
And artour haþ nyw tydynge: — News of Lucius's approach is brought,
Lucy þe Emp*er*our wyþ hys host
Comeþ fast in gret bost;
þey helyþ ouer aƚƚ þe lond,

Fowre hunderd þowsand
An hunderd & foure & twenty,—
Thus herawdes dude ham rekeny ;—
Thus he hadde gadered to hym
Of cristiens and of Sarasyn,
Wyþ aƚƚ hys wytt & labour
To destroyen Arthour.
Arthour dude wyselye,
And hadde euer gode aspye
Of lucyes gouernynge
And of hys þyder comynge ;
But so*m*me seyde hyt wer*e* folye
To fyght aȝenst Emp*erour* lucie,
For he hadde sexe[1] euer*e* aȝenst oon,
& cou*n*ceyled Arth*our* to fle & goon.
Wyþ þe Emp*erour* come kynges Many oon,
And aƚƚ þeire power hooƚƚ & soom ;
Stronger men Myȝt no man see,
As fuƚƚ of drede as þey myght be ;
But / Arthour was nat dysmayd,
He tryst on god, & was wel payd,
And prayd þe hye trynyte
Euer hys help forto be ;
And aƚƚ hys Men wyþ oo voyse
Cryede to god wyþ Oo noyse,
"Fader in heuene, þy wyƚƚ be doon ;
Defende þy puple fram þeire foon,
And lat nat þe heþoñ Men
Destroye þe puple crystien :
Haue Mercy on þy se[r]uañtis bonde,
And kepe ham fram þe heþoñ honde ;

with an army of 400,124 men.

Some advise Arthur to turn and flee,

[leaf 45, col. 2.]

but he trusts in God,

to whom his soldiers pray

to keep them from the heathen's hands.

[1] I read this *sepe* before; but now I read it *sexe ;* for though the *x* is not like that of *ax*, l. 85, or of *axes*, l. 463, Maxymyan, 507, next 508, Saxoynes, 521, &c., yet it is something like that of the 'Xristianitas durat' of the headlines of the English pages, and the 'Destruct*io* x*ri*anitat*is*' of the headline on the back of leaf 46, and Sexaginta, leaf 66, back. But as Arthur had 200,000, and Lucius only 400,124, *sexe* should be *two*.

þe Muchelnesse of Men sainfayle
Ys nat victorie in Batayle;
But after þe wyll þat in heuene ys,
So þe victorie falleþ y-wys."
Than seyd Arthour, "hyt ys so:
Auañt Baner, & be Goo."
Now frendes all, for goddes loue,
Rereþ ȝowre hertes to god aboue,
And seyeþ ȝowre prayeris faste,
þat we well spede furst & laste.

¶ **Pater noster.**

The emperour tryst on hys men,
And þat haþ bygyled hym;
Forsothe hyt most nedeȝ be so,
For þey beþ cursed þat well hyt do,
Such all myght comeþ of god;
To tryst on hym, y hold hyt good,
Lucye haþ pyght his paueloñ
And sprad wyþ pryde his gunfanoñ;
His claryoñs blastes full grete blywe,
Archeris schot (:) Men ouer-thrywe;
Bowes, arwes, & arblastere
Schot sore all y-vere;
Quarels, arwes, þey fly smerte;
þe fyched Men þruȝ heed & herte;
Axes, sperys, and gysarmes gret,
Clefte Many a prowt Mannes heed:
Hors & steedes gan to grent,
And deyde wyþ strokis þat þey hente;
Many a man þere lost hys lyf,
Many on was wedyw þat was wyff;
þere men were wetschoede
All of Brayn & of blode;
Gret rywth hyt was to seyn
þe feltes full of men y-sceyn;
Lucy þe Emperour also was dede;

Arthur's "Forward!"

Maledictus qui confidet in homine.

The battle begins.

[leaf 45, back.]

Men are wetshod with brains and blood.

Lucius is slain,

But ho hym sclowh, y can nat rede;
He, for aƚƚ hys grete Renou*n*,
Aȝenst Arthour hadde no fusou*n*,
No more þan haue twenty schep
Aȝenst vyve wolfeȝ greet.
To god be euere alle hono*ur*eȝ!
The falde was hys & Arthoureȝ.
Arthour, as he scholde done,
Sende lucyes body to Rome.
Whan þe Romeynes say þis,
þo þey dradde Artho*ur* & hys.
Also he buryed Bedewere
Hys frend and / hys Botyler,
And so he dude other Echon
In Abbeys of Relygyon̄
þat were cristien of name;
He dude to alle þe same;
And dude for ham Masse synge
W*yth* sole*m*pne song & offrynge,
And bood þere for to rest
Tyƚƚ þat wynter was past,
Boþe he (.) hys Men echone
Seruyd god in deuocione,
þankyng god of hys Myȝt
þat kepeþ hys serua*u*ntez ryȝt,
And suffreþ noon for to spylle
þ*at* hym loueþ & tryste wylle:
þus worschup god dude certeyn
To Englond, þat þo was Bretayn;
þe More Breteyn Englond ys—
As men may rede on Cronyclys—
Byȝend þe See Bretayne þ*er* ys,
þat haþ hys name forsoþe of þis,
For þe kyng Maxymyan,—
þe next after Octauyan,—
He conquered aƚƚ Armoryk,

not able to stand against Arthur.

Arthur sends Lucius's body to Rome,

buries Bedwere and others

in Abbeys,

and stays the winter,

thanking God

for His honour to England.
[Of the difference between More (or Great) Britain, and Little Britain.]

Quomodo anglia est Britannia maior, & quare maior

[lf. 45 bk, col. 2.]

And to þe Reme named hyt lyk :
Armorica.
Amorica on latyn me cleped þ*a*t lond,
Tyl Maxymyan co[*n*]queryd hyt wy*th* honde,
And called hyt lyte bretayne þan,
So hyȝt þis lond þat he coom fram ;
Little Britain is called after Great Britain.
For p*er*petueƚƚ Mynde of grete Bretayne
He called hyt lyte Bretayne,
þat Men schulde kepe in Mynde & wytt
How þis lond conqueryd hytt ;
For Walscħ Men beþ Bretou*n*s of kynde—
Know þat weƚƚ fast on Mynde—
Englyscħ men beþ Saxoynes,
þ*a*t beþ of Engistes Soones ;
There-fore þe walsch man Bretoñ
Seyþ & clepeþ vs "Sayson" þat ys to seye vpon a reess, "Stynkyng Saxone, be on pees."
How the Welshmen call the English "stinking Saxons."
And seyþ (.) "taw or (.) Peyd Sayson brou*nt*" [1]
Whan he ys wroth (:) or ellys dro*u*nke ;
Hauyng Mynde of Engystis Men
þat wy*th* gyle sclow þeyre kyn :
At þe place of þe Stonehenge
Ȝut þey þenkeþ for to venge :
And þat hyt neuere be so,
Seyþ a Pater noster more to.

¶ Pater noster.

Arthur is preparing to cross the mountains to Rome,
Now turne we to oure labo*ur*,
And lat vs speke of Arthour :
He cast on herte sone
After þat to go to Rome,
And spak of Passage & hys wey
Forth ouer Moñt Ioye.
when he hears of Mordred's treachery ;
And sone after vpon an owr
He hurde of Mordred the treto*ur*

[1] Pughe's abridged Dictionary gives *tau, v.a.* be still ; *taw, s.m.* and *adj.* quiet, silence, silent ; *paid, s.m.* a cessation, quiet ; *bront, a.* nasty, filthy, surly. *Or*, says Dr. Benj. Davies, you must take as equal to the modern Welsh *wr*, man, if it is not English ; *peyd* is cease, pause ; *taw*, be silent.

That hadde aƚƚ þis lond on warde—
Euyƚƚ moot sucħ fare, and harde!
Who may best bygyle a man
But sucħ as he tryst vpan?
þer ys no man wel nye, y tryste,
þat can be waar of hadde wyste.—
Mordred, þis falss Man,
Mucħ sorw þo bygan;
He stuffed alle castells
Wyþ armyre & vytells,
And strenghthed hym on eche syde
W*yth* Men of contreys ferre & wyde: [leaf 46.]
He toke þe qweene, Arthoureȝ wyff, *how the traitor had seized the queen, his (Arthur's) wife,*
Aȝenst goddes lawe & gode lyff,
And putte heore to soiourne þo
At Euerwyk (:) god ȝyf hym̄ wo.—
Yhork ys Euerwyk (:) *and put her at York.*
& so me calleþ hyt.—
Artho*ur* aryved at Whytsond *Arthur then comes home,*
W*yth* gret Myght & strong hond,
And Mordred sainȝ fayl *fights Mordred,*
ȝaf hym þo a strong batayl;
Many a man, as y rede,
þat day was þere dede;
Arthoures nevew Waweyn
þat day was þere y-sclayn, *and Gawain is slain.*
And oþer knyȝtes Many moo:
þan Arthour was heuy & woo.
Mordred fly toward Londou*n*; *Mordred flies to London,*
He most nat come in þe tou*n*:
þan fled he to Wy*n*chester
And w*yth* hys Mayne kep hym þer';
And Arthour on gret haste
Pursywed after hym faste.
Mordred w*ythout*e fayle
Fled in-to Corneways. *and then to Cornwall.*

The qwene wyþoute lesyng
Hurde of þis tydyng,
And how Mordred was flow,
And how to Cornewale he hym drow.
Heo of Mercy hadde noon hoope,
Ther-for he dude on a Russet cote,

The Queen turns nun at Carlyon.

And to Carlyoñ ys preuyly Roñne,
And made heore self þo a Noñne;
Fro þat place neuer heo wende,
But of heore lyf þere made an ende.

Gawain is buried in Scotland.

Waweynes body, as y reede,
And other lordes þat weere deede,
Arthour sente in-to skotlonde,
And buryed ham þ*er*e, y vnd*er*stonde.
Muche folke þ*er*henne he toke þo,

Northern men and others come to Arthur.

Of Northu*m*ber-lond also
Fram dyverse places to Artho*ur* come
Hys wyłł to werk & to done:
Thus he sembled a fułł gret Ost;
To Corneweyle he draweþ hym fast
After þat Mordred þe trayto*ur*
þat hadde do hym Much̄ dyshono*ur*.

[leaf 46, col. 2.]

That treto*ur* hadde gret Strength
And fulled þ*at* lond on brede & length̄,

He gives Mordred battle.

Such̄ a batełł as þere was redy þo
Hadde neuer Arthour byfore y-doo:
They fow3t tyl þer come dou*n* bloode

Bellum arthuri apud Camelertonum in Cornubia.

As a(.) Ryver or (.)a(.) flood;
þey fow3t euer sore & sadde;
Men nyst ho þe betere hadde;
But at þe last Certeyn

Mordred is slain, Arthur wounded, and carried to Avelon, or **Auelona .i. insula pomoru*m* Glastonia.**

Was Mordred & alle hys y-sclayn;
And Artho*ur* y-bete wyþ wou*n*de,
He Myght not stonde on grou*n*de;
But on lyter ry3t anon
Was brow3t to Aueloñ

þ*a*t was a place fayr & Mury ;
Now hyt hooteþ Glastyngbury.

Glastonbury, where he dies,

Ther Arth*our* þat worthy kyng
Maked hys lyues endyng ;
But for he skaped þ*a*t batell y-wys,
Bretoñs & Cornysch seyeþ þus,
"þat he leuyth ȝut p*ar*de,
And schall come & be a kyng aȝe."
At glastyngbury on þe qweer
þey made Art*oure*ȝ tou*m*be þere,

and is buried, A.D. 542.

And wrote wyth latyn vers þus,
Hic iacet Arthurus, rex quonda*m*, rex que futur*us*.
Thys was þus forsoþe ydone
þe yheer after þe Incarnacione,
Vyf hundred (.) fourty & two.

Anno d*omini* qu*in*gente*simo* quadragesi*mo* sec*un*do.

Now saue vs alle fra woo
Ih*es*u cryst, heuenly kyng,
& grau*n*t vs alle hys blessyng ;
And þat hyt Moote so be,
Seyeþ alle Pater & Aue.
¶ Pater noster / Aue /
Ho þ*a*t woll more loke,
Reed on þe frensch boke,
And he schall fynde þere
þynges þat y leete here.

Read the French Book for the rest.

But yf þat god wolle grau*n*te gr*ace*,
y schall rehercy in þis place
Alle þe kyngez þat after were,
And what names at þey bere ;
And ho þ*a*t woll þeyre gestes loke,
Reed on þe Frensch boke. Amen fiat.

[On the back of leaf 46 follows : 'Destructio *christianitatis* / Et reformacio eiusde*m*. Constantinus. Post Arthuru*m* regnauit Constantin*us*, fili*us* Cador, Comit*is* Cornubie, nepos Arthuri / iste constantin*us* interfecit duos filios Mordredi spurios, qui Moueru*nt* bellu*m* cont*ra* eu*m* p*ro*pt*er* p*at*rem eo*rum*,' &c., &c.]

WORDS.

a, he, l. 370.
alowte, l. 116, bowed down to.
aspye, *sb.* espial, l. 416 ; *vb.* ascertain, ll. 202, 268.
ayhe, again, l. 126.
beeme, *sb.* ? noise, display, from A.S. *béme*, a trumpet, l. 108.
doelle, l. 101, sorrow.
falde, l. 480, felt, l. 472 ; field.
foon, l. 434, foes.
fusoun, gain, victory, l. 476. L. *fusio*, outpouring, plenty ; common in Scotland for 'pith, bottom.'
fyched, pierced, l. 462.
goom, man, l. 166.
gysarme, l. 463. *Hallebarde, pique, hache.* Roquefort.
hadde wyste, l. 546, had I known (how it would have turned out). See Nares, and the Poem "Beware of had-I-wyst," that he quotes. "Beware of *had-I-wyst*, whose fine bringes care and smart."
hawted, exalted, l. 113.
he, she, l. 582.
heo, l. 581, she.
helyth, cover (or pour out, *helĕ* Wilts., *hale* Dorset.), l. 407.
hente, l. 96, took ; l. 466, received.
hulle, l. 399, hill.
last, lest, l. 289.
leete, l. 636, leave, omit.
loghynge, lodging, l. 344.
lynage, descendant, l. 269.
meyntenaunt, l. 383, presently, soon.
muchelnesse, *sb.* muchness, number and power, l. 439.
mynde, remembrance, l. 527.
nyst, l. 606, ne wyst, knew not.
oo, one, l. 49, 135.
pyght, l. 455, pitched.
raply, l. 87, quickly.
rees, l. 524, rush, stir ?
remes, l. 209, realms.
sayle, assail, attack, l. 12.
scley, slain, l. 212.
skyle, *sb.* reason, l. 17.
soueȝ (?), sough, moan, l. 88.
that, ye who, l. 1 ; those who, l. 42, 84.
theoband (l. 178), is, I expect, miswritten for theo*d*and ; A.S. *þeodan*, to join ; *ge-þeod-an*, to join, associate.
therhenne, thence, l. 591.
tho, l. 138, then.
toke, gave, l. 329.
trywage, l. 270, 288, truage, tribute.
venge, have revenge, take vengeance, l. 530.
verrament, truly, l. 32.
was, whose, l. 248.
whas, whose, l. 198, 201.
wocd, wild, mad, l. 211.
ydoon, done, spent, l. 72.
ye, l. 299, eye.
ylete, let, l. 194.
ytake, taken to, given to, l. 272.
y-vere, together, l. 460.
ywyss, certainly, l. 46.

The manufacturer's authorised representative in the EU for product safety is Oxford University Press España S.A. of El Parque Empresarial San Fernando de Henares, Avenida de Castilla, 2 - 28830 Madrid (www.oup.es/en or product.safety@oup.com). OUP España S.A. also acts as importer into Spain of products made by the manufacturer.
Printed and bound by CPI Group (UK) Ltd, Croydon, CR0 4YY
20/03/2026
02075340-0001